What's it Like to Drive?

Keith Gaines

Contents

You will meet these abbreviations in this book:

m means metres

km means kilometres

2

What's it like to drive a car?

Lucy is 18 and she is having driving lessons.

My driving instructor comes to my house in her car.

The car has dual controls. The instructor can use her controls to brake or to speed up the car.

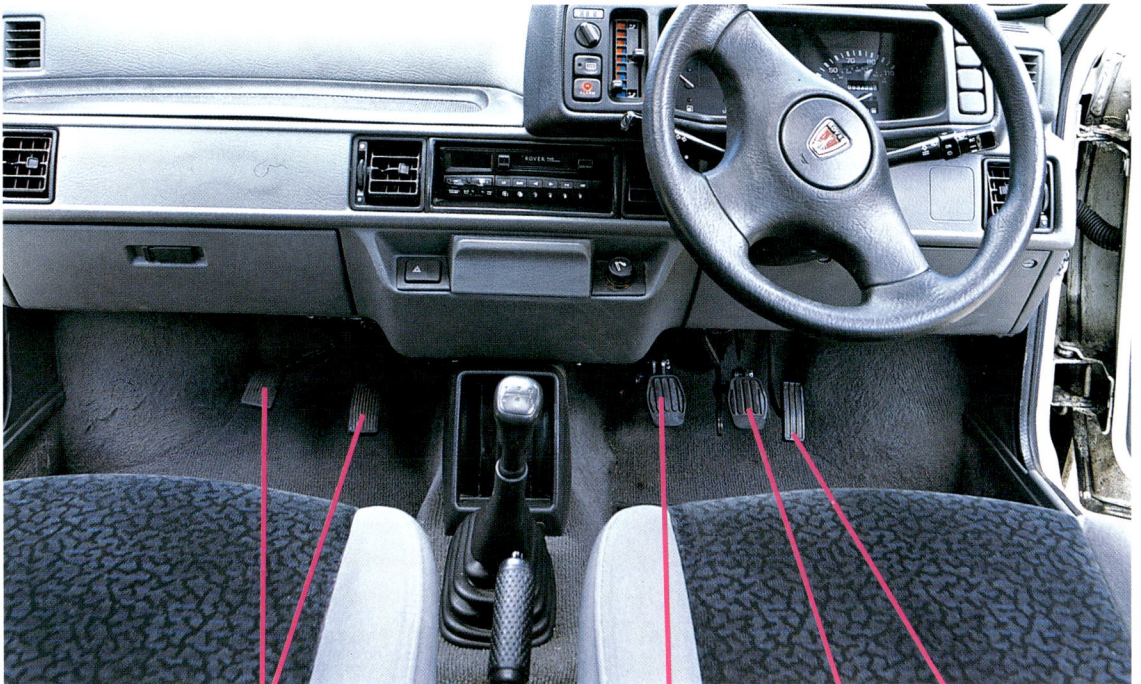

instructor's controls

clutch

brake

fuel

It's hard to remember all the things you have to do:

- turn the steering wheel
- look in the mirrors for other traffic
- use indicators when turning
- use the handbrake
- keep under the speed limit.

The driver's controls

mirrors

hazard light

speed dial

indicator switch

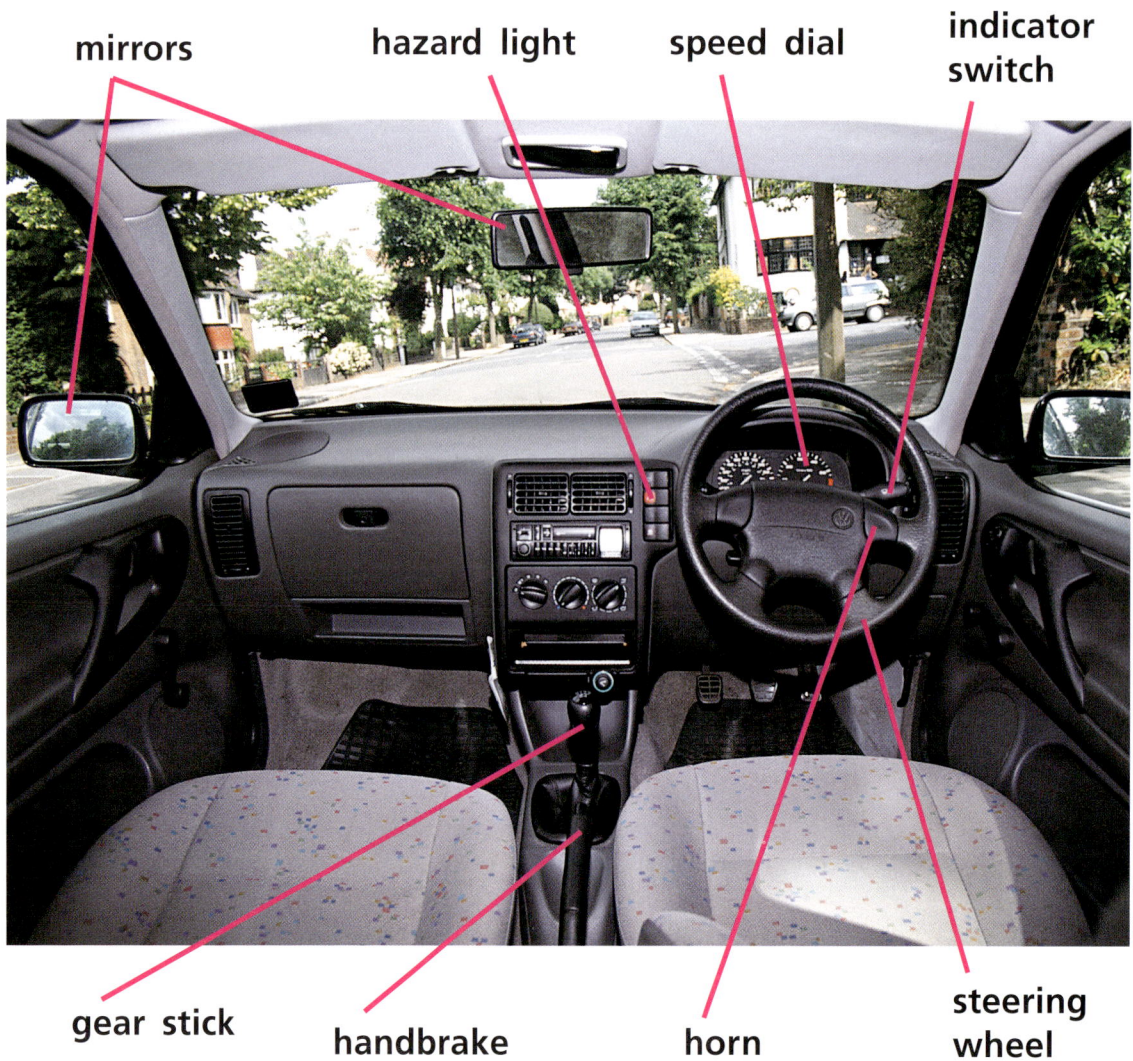

gear stick

handbrake

horn

steering wheel

At the same time, I have to change gear when the car changes speed.

Changing gear

clutch pedal

1 Push down the clutch pedal.

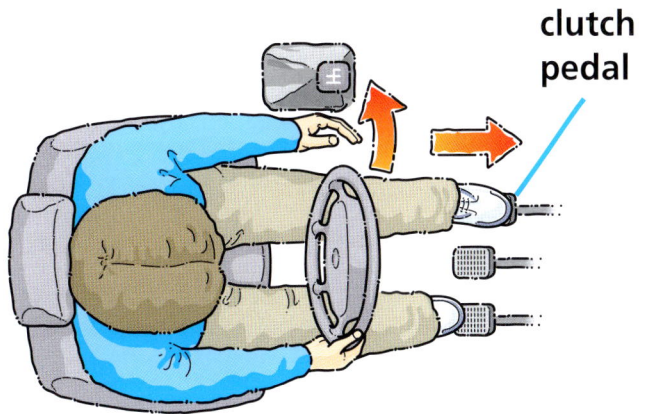

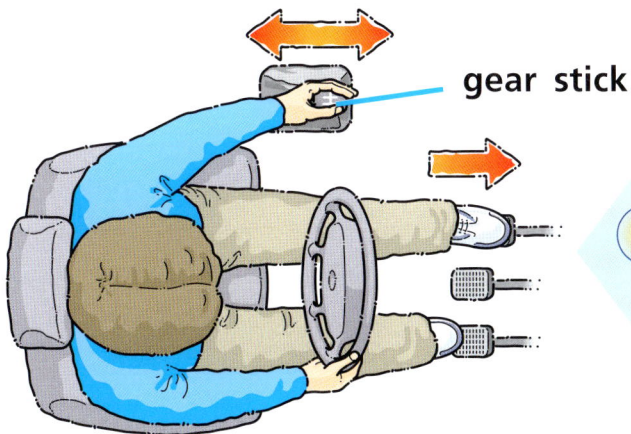

gear stick

2 Move the gear stick to a new gear.

3 Let the clutch pedal come up.

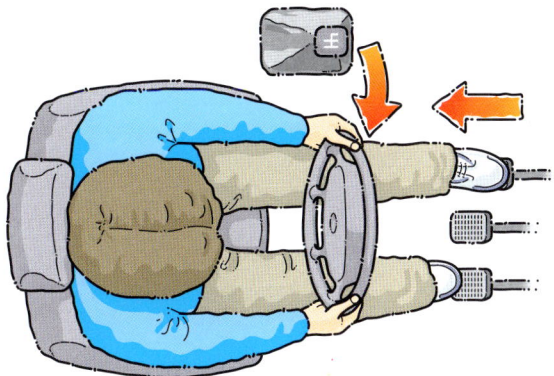

What's it like to drive a bus?

Leroy has been a bus driver for 12 years.

There are two big differences between driving a bus and a car. One is that a bus is much bigger, so the driver has to learn how to handle such a large vehicle.

Bus drivers have to pass a special bus-driving test.

The other difference is that all modern buses have power steering. You can turn the steering wheel with just your finger!

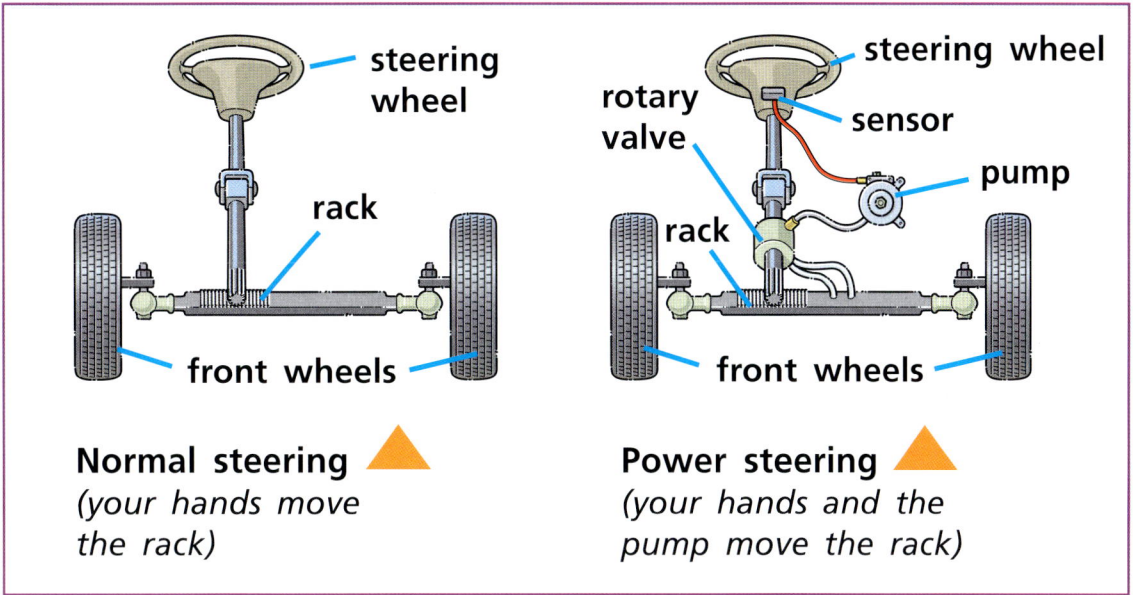

steering wheel

rotary valve

sensor

pump

rack

rack

front wheels

front wheels

Normal steering
(your hands move the rack)

Power steering
(your hands and the pump move the rack)

In town traffic, buses often have to drive through narrow spaces.

I prefer driving my bus to driving my car.
I like meeting people and I get to know a lot of the regular passengers.

What's it like to drive a lorry?

Dave has been driving lorries for 15 years.

I drive the big lorries we call "artics" – short for "articulated". That means it bends in the middle. This kind of lorry has a cab and a trailer.

Some cabs have beds, so the driver can take a break from a long journey, and sleep.

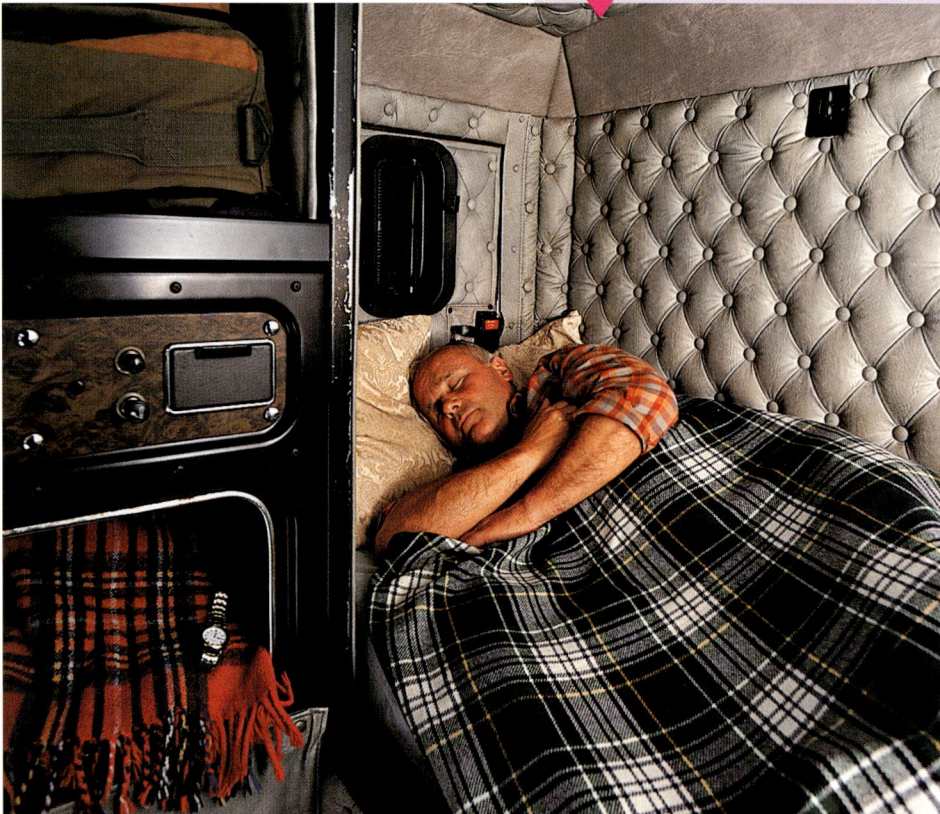

There are different sorts of trailers for different sorts of loads.

A trailer for chilled foods

A trailer for machinery

A trailer for cars

A trailer for containers which can be loaded onto trains or ships

I get to travel all over the country, which I like.
I wouldn't like to drive the same route every day.

What's it like to drive a fire engine?

Darren is 27 and has been in the Fire Service since he left school.

I took two special driving tests to drive the appliance – that's what we call the fire engine. The first test lets me drive an ordinary heavy goods vehicle (HGV). The second test lets me drive fast to an emergency.

When there is an accident on the motorway, firefighters need to drive fast, but also carefully.

To pass the second test I learnt how to drive:

- through red lights
- through lots of traffic
- on the wrong side of the road.

Most of the time I drive normally. This morning we rescued a bird tangled up in a tree. It's not all racing through red lights in the Fire Service!

The bird was here.

FIRE-RESCUE is written backwards, so drivers can read it in their mirrors.

What's it like to drive a JCB?

Harry has worked in building for 28 years.

I can drive any kind of van or lorry, dumper truck, caterpillar truck, mobile crane or JCB.

JCBs are tricky to work because there are so many levers to control the shovel.

We use the shovel for scooping up stuff and getting the ground level. We use the digging arm to dig trenches for water pipes.

JCBs are made by J. C. Bamford, and that's where they got their name from.

digging arm

JCB

shovel

digger

Caterpillar tracks run easily over wet or rough ground.

What's it like to drive a dumper truck?

Helen has worked as a dumper truck driver for four years.

The tricky thing about small dumper trucks is that you steer them with the back wheels, although you turn the steering wheel the same way as when you drive a car.

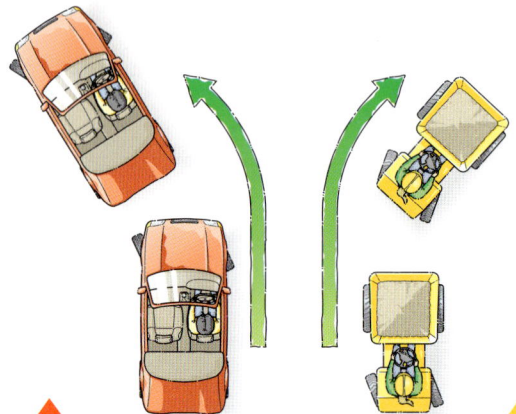

A car is steered with front wheels.

A dumper is steered with back wheels.

The tyres of a dumper truck are thick with deep treads for grip.

Sometimes I drive on the road, but mostly I drive on a building site. The dumper's a tough truck and it can go over pretty rough ground. We use it for carrying bricks and for moving rubbish.

What's it like to drive a crane?

Mark has been a crane-driver for 13 years.

Most of my work is on big building sites, like for new office blocks. Sometimes I work on bridges. A few years ago I worked on a site for a big dam in Africa.

Some cranes are taken to a site in bits. Then they are put together. Other cranes are mobile units – they fold out from lorries.

A mobile crane

pulley   arm   cab   weight

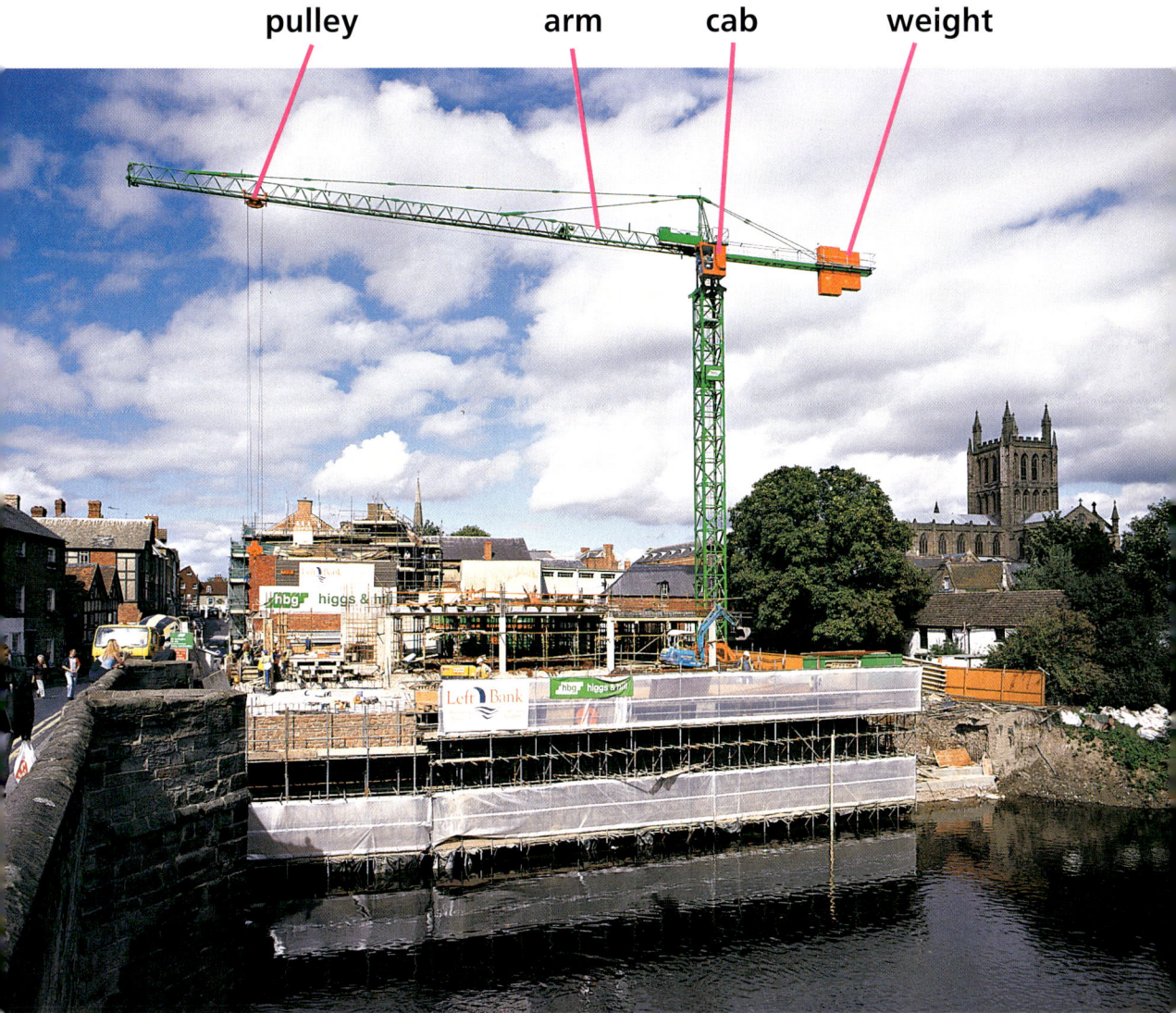

I sit in the cab and work the levers. These make the lifting gear move up and down, and move it along the arm of the crane.

The best bit of the job is the terrific views you get from so high up. The worst bit is getting to work – climbing up to the cab!

What's it like to drive a train?

Mick drives Intercity trains.

I drive the express from London to Preston. It's a push-pull train – with an engine at each end.

The controls in a train are simple, but you have to know hundreds of railway rules and be alert all the time.

An Intercity express train

18

Each bit of the route has to be driven at a set speed. You must obey all the signals and look out for people on the line.

Even when the track ahead looks clear, you can get a big bird suddenly hitting the front window. When you're doing 140 km per hour that makes a big bang!

As you come into a station, you look for signs on the platform. These show you where to stop the train.

The top sign shows the driver where to stop.

You have to get there on time. If you arrive late, you get in trouble. If you arrive early, you get in trouble for speeding!

I can be driving for eleven hours a day.

It's a big responsibility being in charge of a 400-tonne train, travelling at 160 km per hour and full of people.

Every day, millions of people travel by train.

The best bit of the job is the last 100 m into the last station!

Do you know the road signs?

Look at each sign. Write down which answer you think is correct (A, B or C).
Check your answers at the bottom of page 23.

1) A No parking
   B No entry
   C Red cars only

2) A No overtaking
   B Overtake on the left
   C Only red cars can overtake

3) A Cycles only
   B No boys' bikes
   C No cycling

4) A No cars or lorries carrying explosives
   B Warning – exploding cars ahead
   C Only cars with lights on the roof

5) A Free parking all day for cars and bikes
   B No black cars or motorbikes
   C No cars or motorbikes

6) A Turn right ahead
   B Turn left ahead
   C Look left

7) A Bend to left
   B Bend to right
   C No rubber pencils allowed

8) A Uneven road
   B Speed bumps ahead
   C Warning – big stones in road

9) A Sharp bends ahead
   B Drive on the pavement
   C Slippery road

10) A Warning – wild animals
    B Do not overtake deer
    C No entry except for Santa Claus

11) A Do not overtake aircraft
    B Warning – low flying aircraft
    C Jumbo jet landing on road ahead

12) A Sudden drop ahead
    B Wait for bridge to be built
    C Sea or river bank ahead – end of road

Index

526505